TINY SCIENCE

NANOTECHNOLOGY

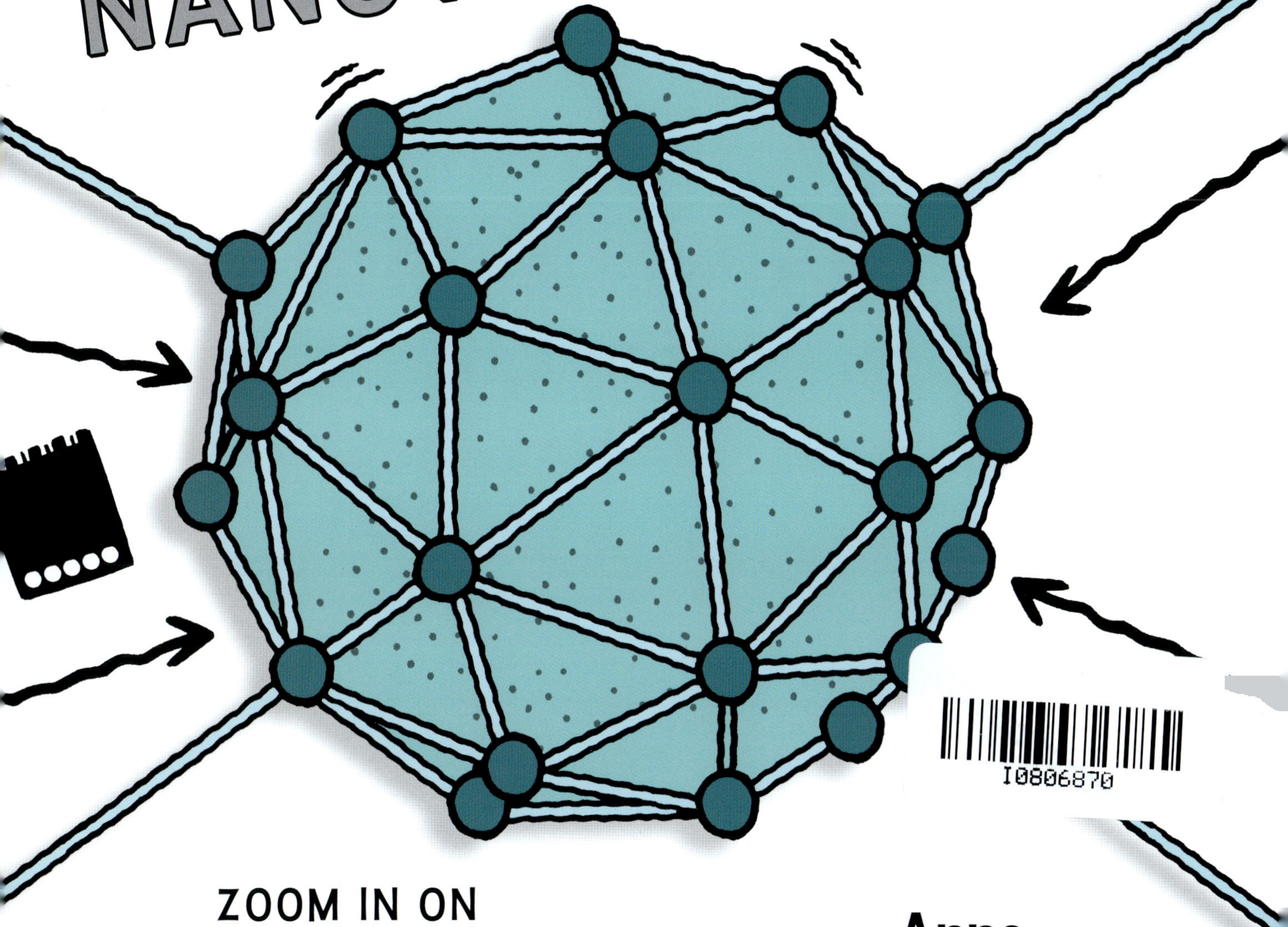

ZOOM IN ON THE TINY TECH AT WORK IN MEDICINE, COMPUTING, ROBOTICS, AND MORE!

Anna Claybourne

Gareth Stevens PUBLISHING

**Please visit our website,
www.garethstevens.com.
For a free color catalog of all
our high-quality books, call
toll free 1-800-542-2595 or
fax 1-877-542-2596.**

Published in 2025 by
Gareth Stevens Publishing
2544 Clinton St.
Buffalo, NY 14224

First published in Great Britain in 2022 by Wayland

Editor:
Grace Glendinning

Design and illustrations:
Matt Lilly

Cover design:
Matt Lilly

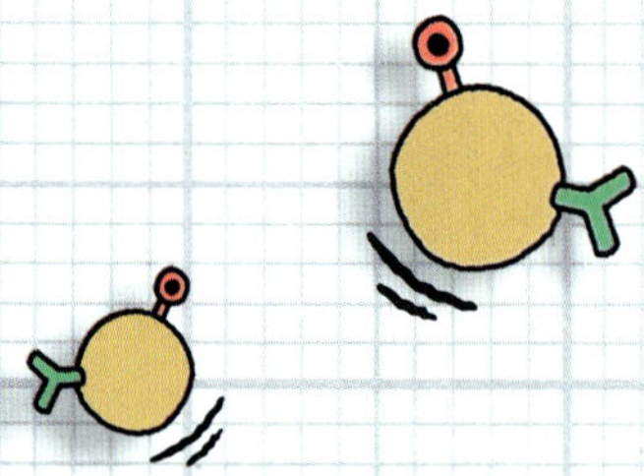

Cataloging-in-Publication Data

Names: Claybourne, Anna.
Title: Nanotechnology / Anna Claybourne.
Description: Buffalo, NY : Gareth Stevens Publishing, 2025. | Series: Tiny science | Includes glossary and index.
Identifiers: ISBN 9781538294208 (pbk.) | ISBN 9781538294215 (library bound) | ISBN 9781538294222 (ebook)
Subjects: LCSH: Nanotechnology--Juvenile literature.
Classification: LCC T174.7 C54 2025 | DDC 620'.5--dc23

Alamy: Agefotostock 25c; Science History Images 6b; Science Photo Library 21b.
A*STAR: Institute of Bioengineering & Technology 15b, 17t.
Dreamstime: Albert Shakirov 17b; Spbphoto 6c.
Science Photo Library: Stefan Diller 24bc; Eye of Science 13tr; Steve Gschmeissner 22br; Franz Himpsel/University of Wisconsin 19b; IBM Research 7c; Alfred Pasieka 5c; Joseph Stroscio, Robert Celotta/National Institute of Standards and Technology 10b.
Shutterstock: Africa Studio 27tr; Digital storm 27tl; DKN0049 5t; Fasttailwind 5b; Miriam Doerr Martin Frommherz 8b; Kolonko 18t; Kateryna Kon 20t, 31b; My Portfolio 12br; Pvince73 24bl; StudioMolekuul 9t.
Wikimedia/PD: Tokyo University 7b.

Printed in the United States of America

CPSIA compliance information: Batch #CSGS25: For further information contact Gareth Stevens at 1-800-542-2595.

Find us on

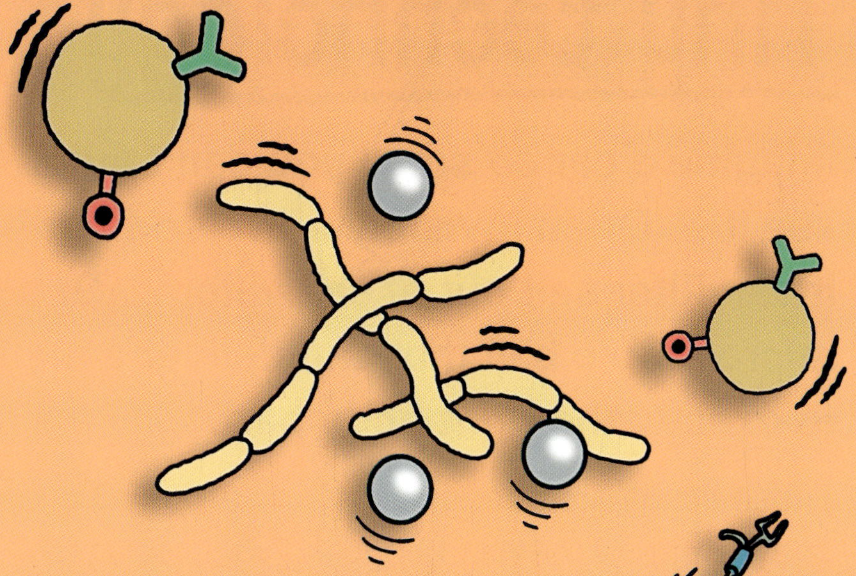

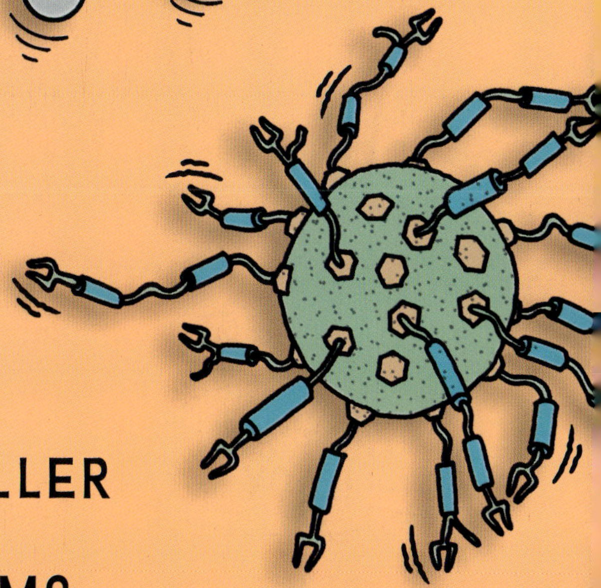

Contents

Tiny technology

Imagine a car so small you can't even see it … Or an invisible sieve so fine that it can filter salt out of seawater … Or a microscopic ball that can deliver a medicine to exactly the right body part.

These things are already here!
They're part of the mind-bogglingly tiny science of …

nanotechnology!

What does "nano" mean?

"Nano" means very, very small – so small, it can be measured in **nanometers**.

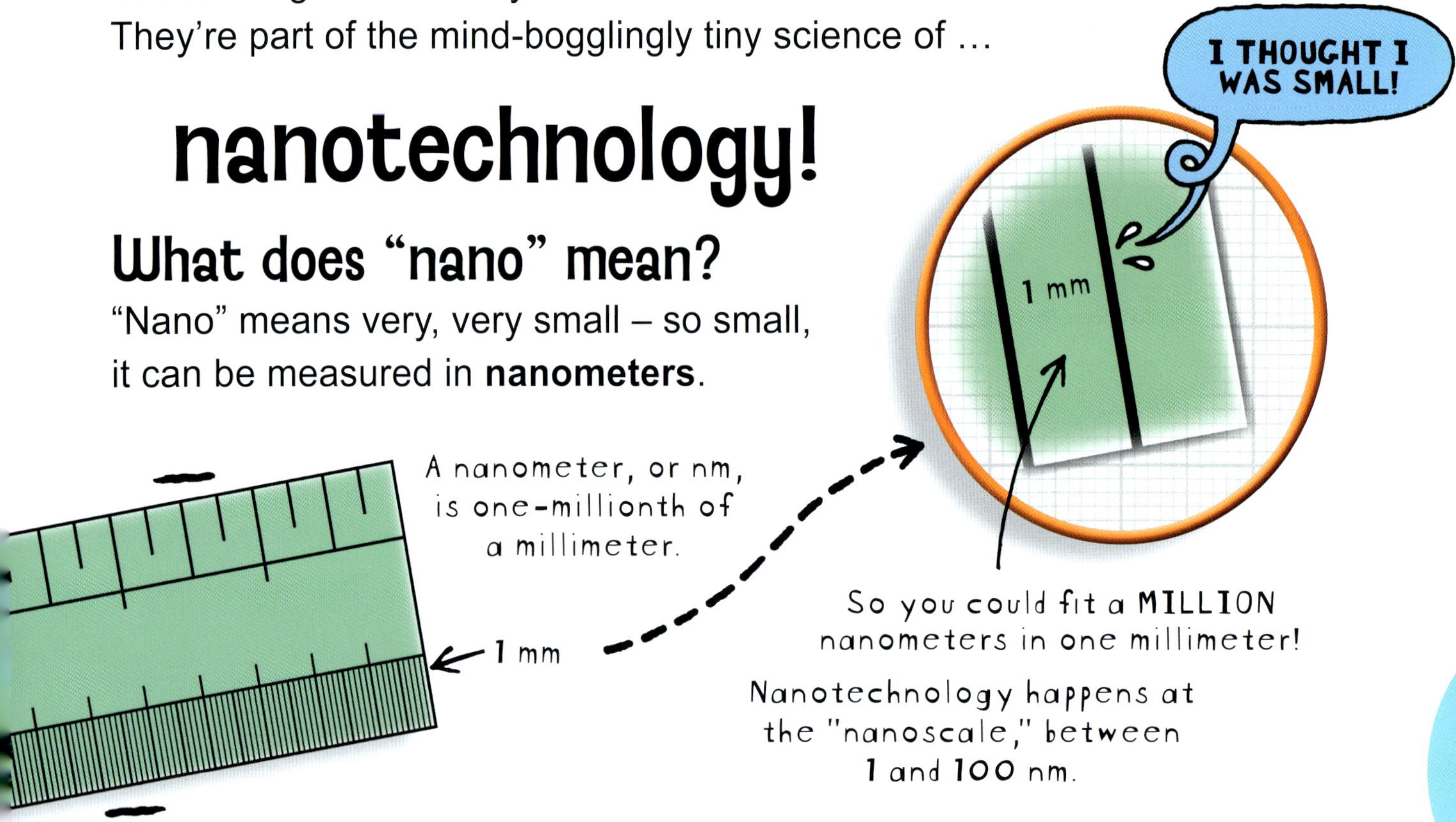

Atoms and molecules

All the stuff, or matter, in the universe is made up of tiny atoms. A typical atom is about 0.1 nm across (or one-tenth of a nanometer).

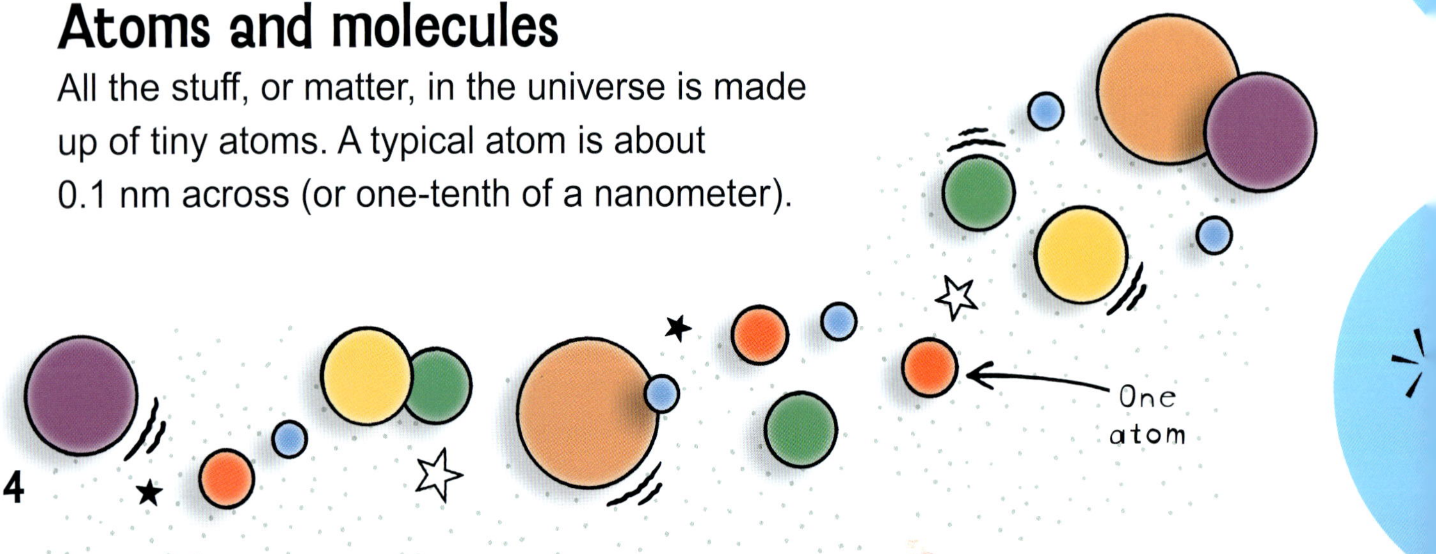

Atoms join up to make larger molecules.

For example, salt is made of molecules, made up of smaller atoms.

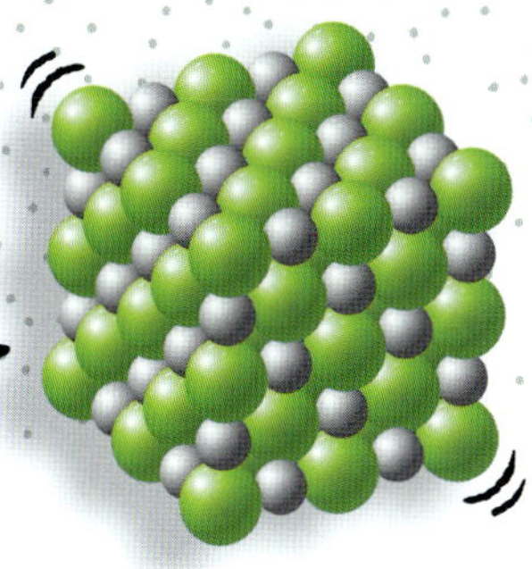

Salt molecules in a crystal structure

In nanotechnology, scientists often work with atoms and molecules. They use them to build and invent things or change them to make new materials.

Under the microscope

This is what a tiny nanocar made of atoms looks like! It has moving parts and really works.

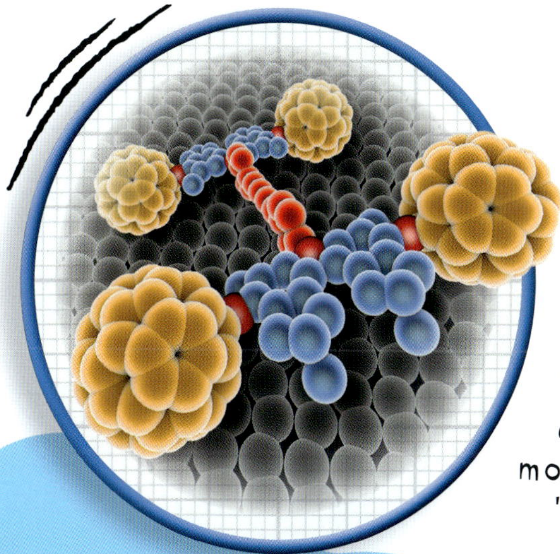

The wheels are made of molecules called "buckyballs."

Nano inventions

Technology can mean computers and machines, but nanotechnology includes many other inventions too. As well as tiny things, it's used to make parts of bigger things.

And that's just the start! Turn the page to find out more ...

Smaller and smaller

Nanotechnology is quite new – it has only existed since the 1980s.

That might sound ancient, but other types of science are **MUCH** older. For example, astronomy, the study of the stars, is thousands of years old.

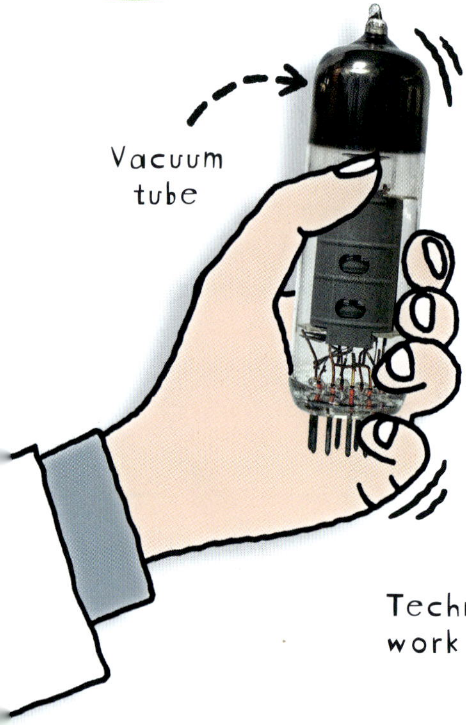

Vacuum tube

So how did nanotechnology begin?

In the 1940s, scientists built the first electric computers. They contained glass vacuum tubes, which did calculations by switching an electric current on and off.

ENIAC, an early computer built in the 1940s, contained over 17,000 vacuum tubes and took up as much floor space as 5 buses!

Technicians at work on ENIAC

In 1947, the transistor was invented to replace the vacuum tube in computers. It was made of metal and was much smaller – and computers began to shrink.

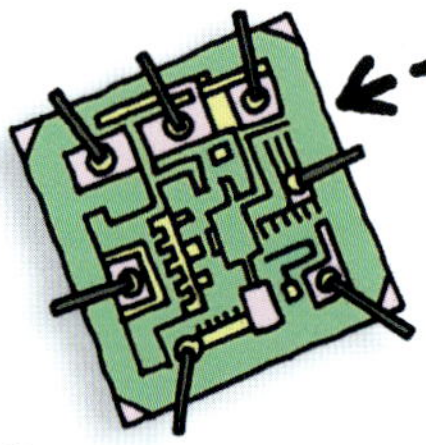

By the 1960s, computers were made using tiny silicon chips.

Under the microscope

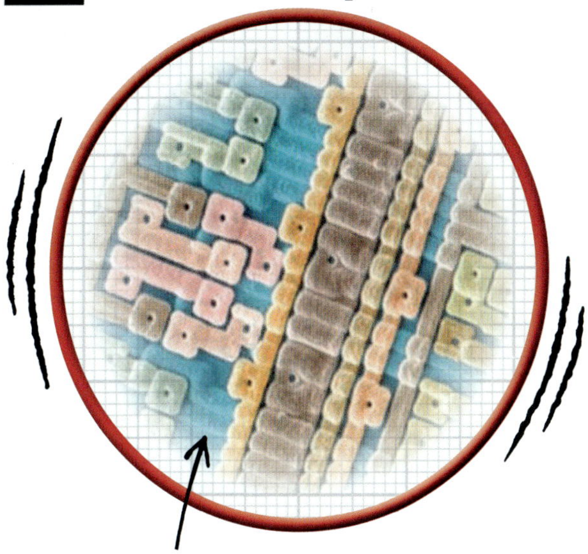

A silicon chip has tiny circuits on it, made by printing thin layers of metal.

Understanding atoms

Meanwhile, scientists discovered more about how atoms work. By the 1950s, we could see atoms by using the latest microscopes. And in the 1980s, a new type of microscope allowed scientists to move atoms around and arrange them into shapes.

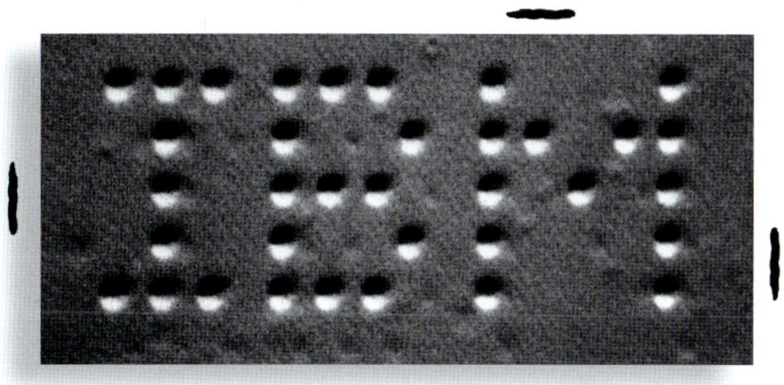

Scientists made this IBM logo out of atoms in 1989. The whole logo is just 3 nm wide.

Nanotech is the future!

In 1959, the famous scientist Richard Feynman predicted nanotechnology, saying we would eventually be able to make microscopic things.

And in 1986, a book called *Engines of Creation*, by engineer K. Eric Drexler, described lots of things that the new science of nanotechnology could do, such as building tiny machines, making medicines, and storing data.

Since then, nanotechnology has taken off.

A Japanese scientist, Norio Taniguchi, came up with the name "nanotechnology" in 1974.

Nano nature

Nanotechnology is a new science, but tiny things themselves are not new!

World of atoms

Everything is made of nano-sized atoms and molecules. That includes Earth and all its rocks, water, plants, animals, and other living things. And all around us, things that occur at the nanoscale control how materials, objects, and living things work.

Ever wondered why ice floats?

When water freezes, its molecules form a network and spread apart slightly. That makes ice lighter for its size than water, and that's why it floats.

How does a pencil make a mark?

Pencil lead contains graphite, a soft, black mineral made of carbon atoms. The atoms are arranged in flat molecules that form layers.

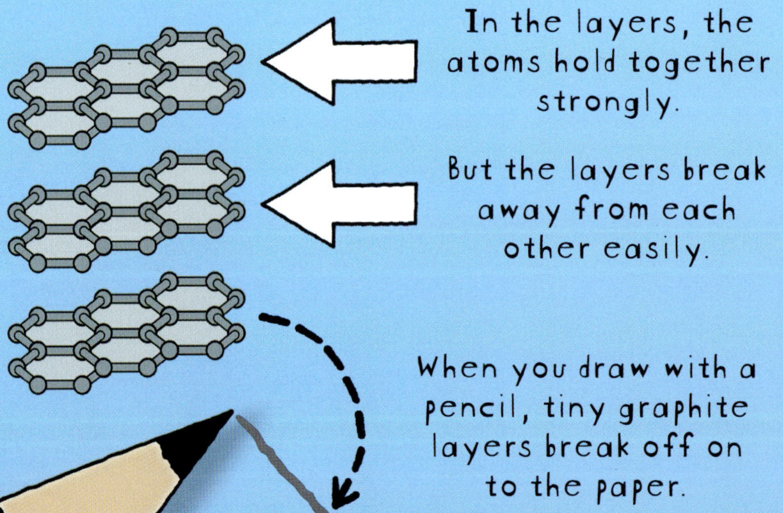

Cells at work

Living things are made up of microscopic cells. Inside cells, tiny parts called organelles move molecules around and use them to build useful materials, such as new cells, fingernails, feathers, or bone.

Hair follicles in your scalp build keratin molecules to make hair.

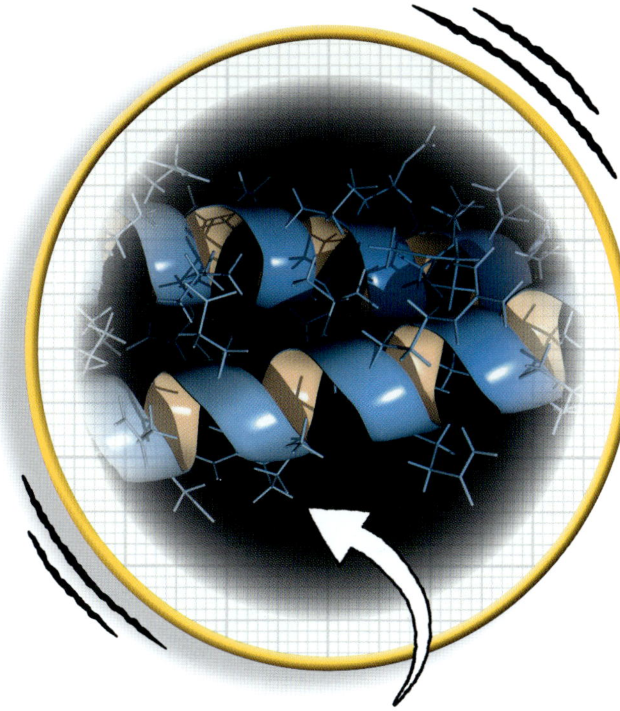

The spiral shape of the molecules in hair makes it slightly stretchy.

Bacteria-killing nanowings

Some cicadas (a type of insect) have wings covered in nano-sized spikes, or "nanopillars," that can destroy bacteria that land on them.

We can do that!

Nanoscientists often use natural nano effects as inspiration. For example, they've made medical tools with a bacteria-killing surface by copying the cicada's nanopillars.

Working with atoms

In 1989, scientists figured out how to move atoms around and rearrange them. This was BIG news in science!

WHY? Because it was the first step toward being able to make anything we want, just by building it out of the right atoms.

However, we can't quite replicate things instantly yet because it's very hard to do. Scientists have found several different methods . . .

Method 1: Micro mover

The first method, used in 1989, uses a scanning tunneling microscope, or STM.

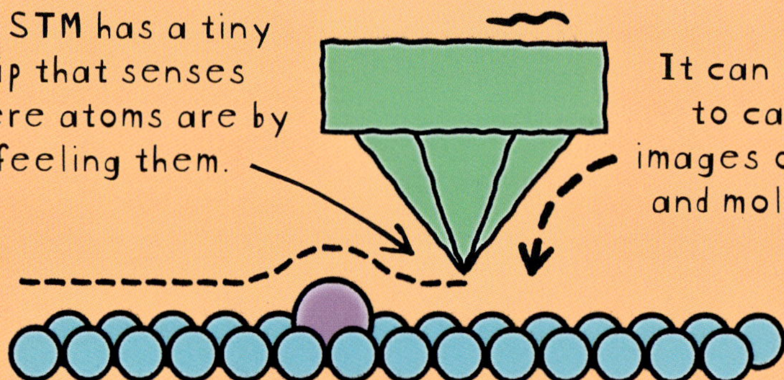

Under the microscope

Scientists also found they could use the tip to pick up and move atoms around on a surface.

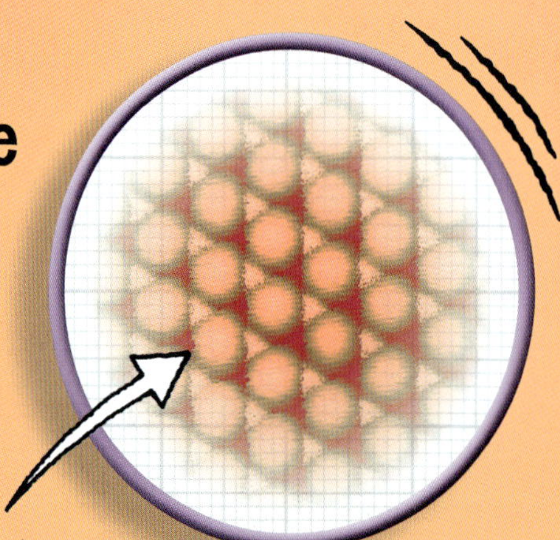

An STM picture of copper atoms

By combining different atoms, you can build tiny nano objects and machines, such as nanocars.

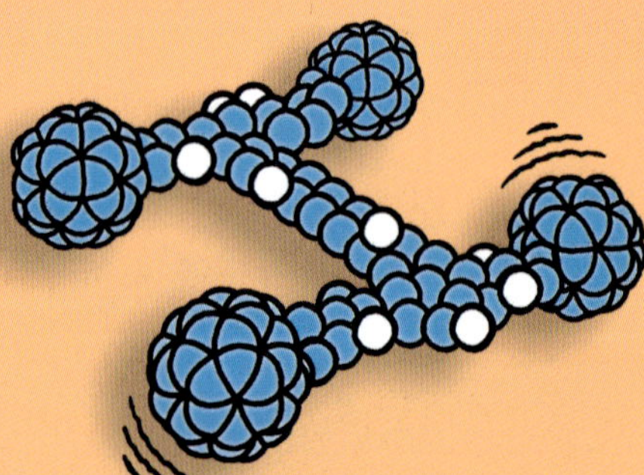

On your marks, get set ...

In 2017, nanoscientists from around the world held the first nanocar race to show off their molecule-building skills.

The winning car reached a blistering 300 nm per hour. (At that speed, it would take 380 years to travel 3 feet [1 meter], so the race was not, in fact, held on a road!)

Method 2: 3D printer

Another way to build with atoms is to shoot them at a surface to form layers. Gradually they build up into a 3D object.

It's just like a tiny 3D printer!

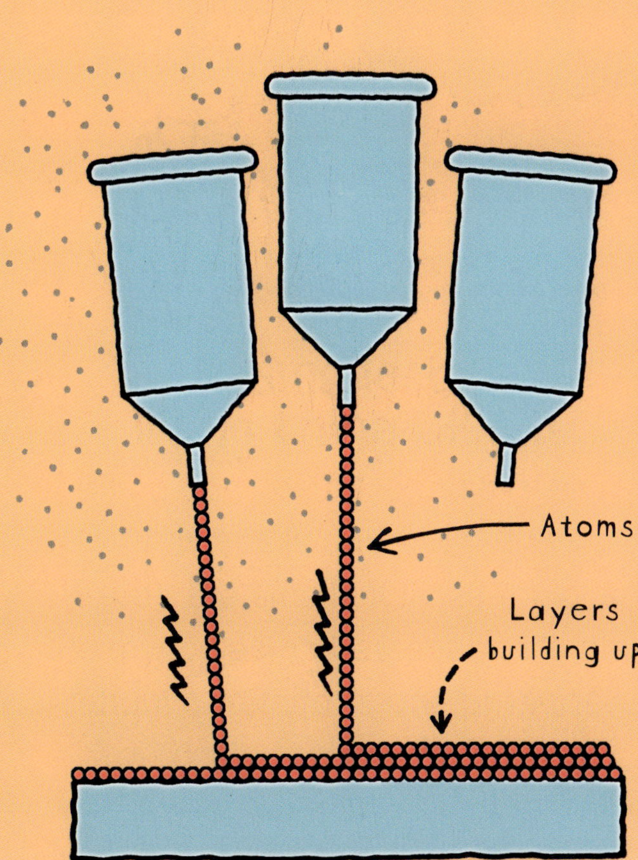

Method 3: Building blocks

Or you can make small molecules that work like bricks and naturally fit or snap together when you combine them.

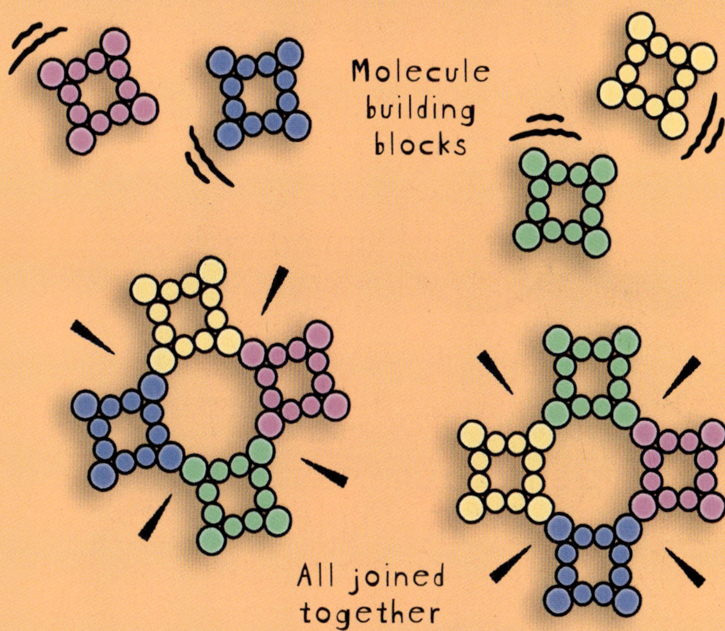

We could use this to make things like vaccines or replacement body parts.

Mini materials

Have you used nanotechnology? Probably! There are nano-sized substances, or nanomaterials, in lots of everyday stuff.

What are they like?

Nanomaterials come in several forms:

Nanofilms are thin, flat sheets, less than 100 nm thick.

Nanotubes and **nanowires** are string-shaped and less than 100 nm wide.

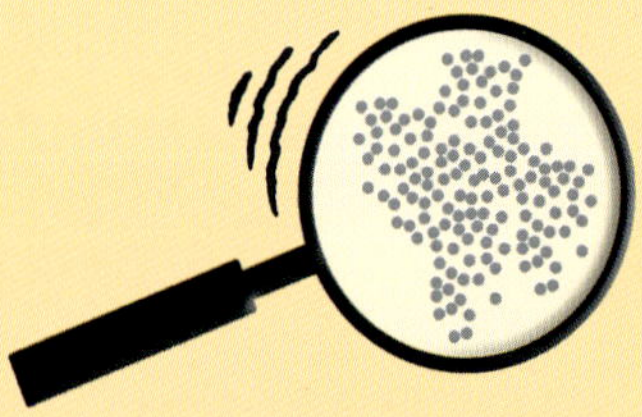

Nanoparticles are tiny specks. They're nano-sized in all directions!

Cool carbon

Nanomaterials can be made of metals, plastics, and many other substances. Carbon makes especially good nanomaterials. It's the same stuff that graphite is made of (see page 8).

Graphene is a flat layer, or nanofilm, of carbon, one atom thick.

It's so thin it's invisible, but it's super strong, light, flexible, and waterproof, and it conducts electricity.

It's used in things like protective helmets, bendy phone screens, and waterproof coatings.

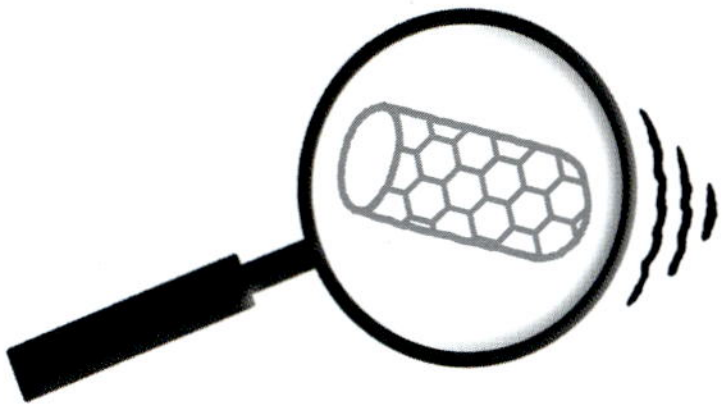

Under the microscope

Carbon nanotubes are made of graphene in a rolled-up tube shape.

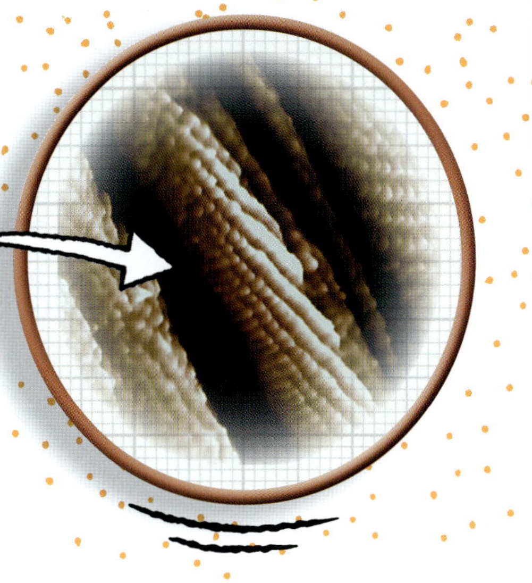

A microscope image of carbon nanotubes

They're stronger than diamond, but bendy like rubber. Combined with plastics, they create incredibly light, strong materials, used in …

Bikes

Skis

Plane wings

Tennis rackets

Wind turbine blades

Buckyballs are carbon nanoparticles, made of carbon atoms in a ball shape.

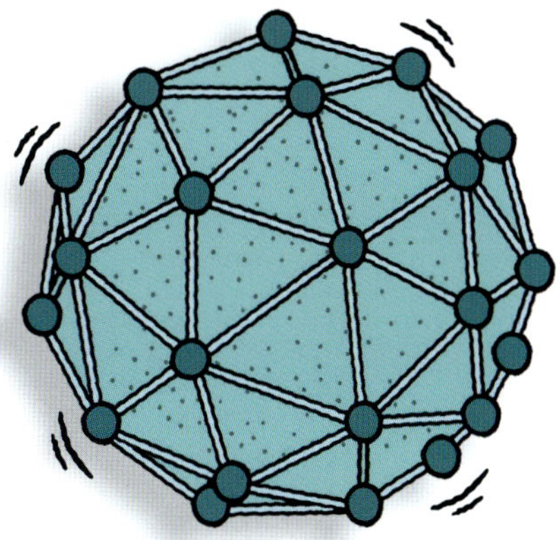

A buckyball can hold smaller molecules inside it. So it can be used to store other substances or as a nanocapsule to deliver medicines inside the body.

Sunscreen, socks, and solar power

And there's more …

Nanoparticles of titanium dioxide in sunscreen absorb dangerous UV light but are so small they are see-through.

Silver nanoparticles kill bacteria. They are embedded into socks to make them less smelly!

Nanofilms are being used to make very thin, light, flexible solar panels.

Nanoclay containing nanoparticles stops air from leaking out of tennis balls, making them stay bouncy!

Nano cleanup

We live in a world full of dirt, dust, and pollution, which are often very hard to clean up. But nanotechnology has all kinds of clever cleaning tricks ...

Self-cleaning windows

Glass skyscrapers are beautiful, but they need a lot of cleaning.

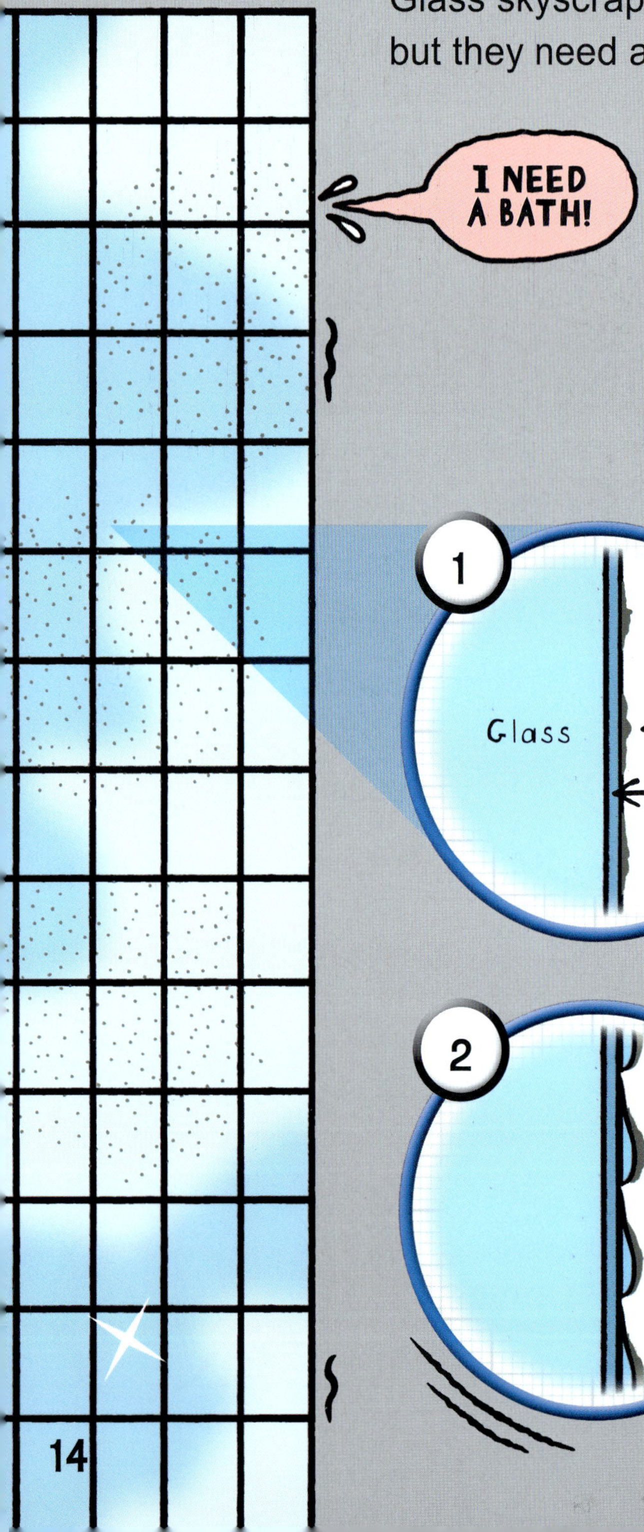

So nanoscientists have invented glass that can clean itself. It's coated with a nanomaterial made of titanium dioxide (the same stuff that's used in sunscreen).

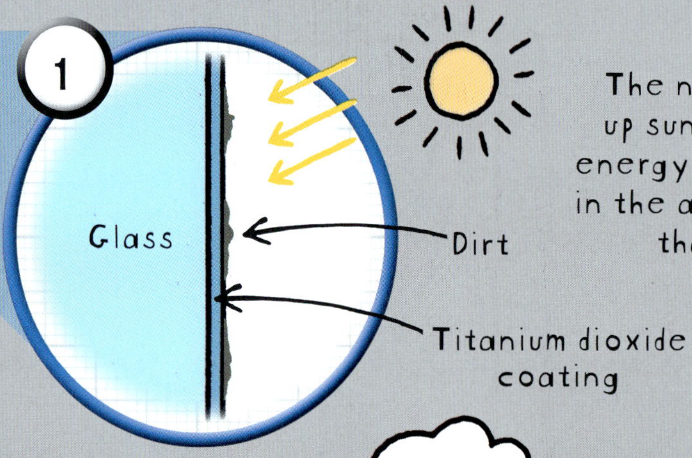

The nanomaterial soaks up sunlight. It uses light energy to react with water in the air, making chemicals that break up dirt.

The nanomaterial attracts water. So when it rains, water sticks to the glass, pushing the broken-up dirt away.

Oil-spill solutions

When a tanker spills oil, it's very hard to clean up because the oil is so thick and sticky.

Oil spills can harm seabirds by covering them in oil and clogging up their feathers.

To fix this, we can use nanomaterials that repel, or push away, water. Here are two genius methods:

Magnetic method:

These water-repelling nanoparticles contain iron. In the sea, they repel water, so only oil sticks to them.

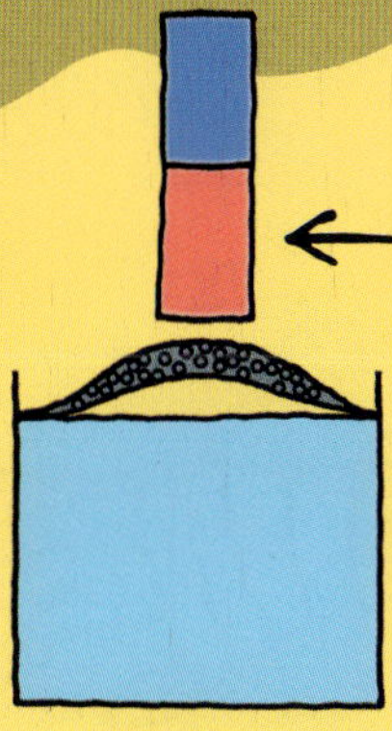

Then a big magnet can collect them, along with all the oil!

Nanosponge method:

This invention is a kind of mat made of millions of tiny water-repelling nanowires.

They push the water away and soak up the oil like a sponge.

The mat can even be cleaned and reused.

Clean drinking water

Many people around the world don't have clean water. A nanotechnology filter, made from layers of graphene, could be the answer.

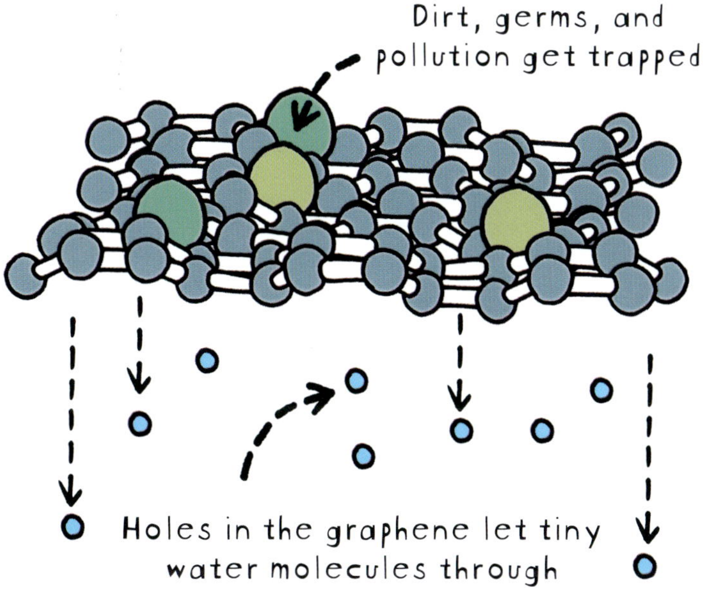

Nanomedicine

Inside our bodies, our cells and blood and disease germs are made of tiny nano-sized parts. So, nanotechnology can work really well to fix health problems – in lots of ways!

Some of these examples exist already ... Others are on the way.

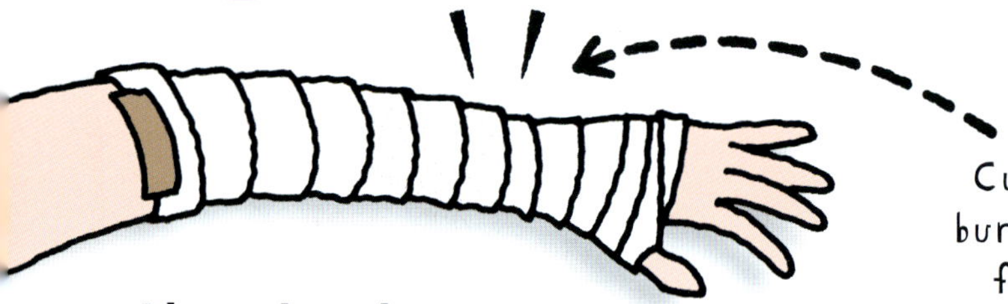

Nano bandages

Adding silver nanoparticles to bandages kills germs.

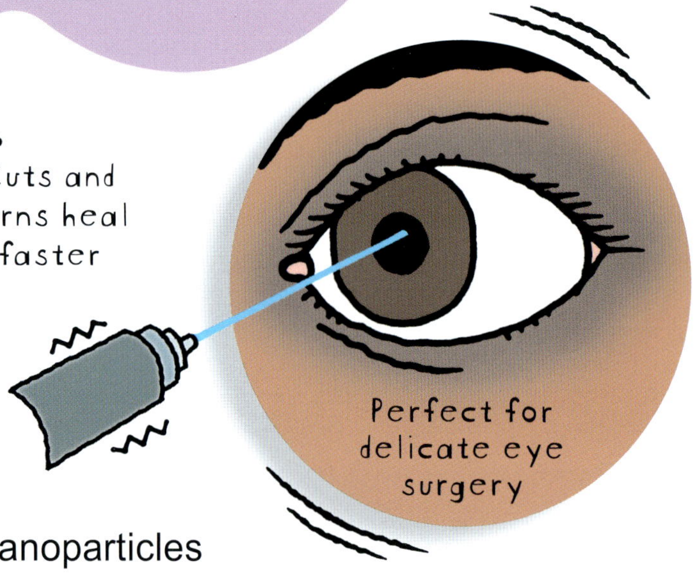

Nano laser scalpel

This new laser device uses gold nanoparticles to focus a laser into a tiny cutting beam. It can make very fine incisions without damaging nearby cells.

No more stitches!

Instead of stitching up a cut, it can be glued with a gel containing nanoparticles of silica (similar to sand) or rust – both harmless to the body.

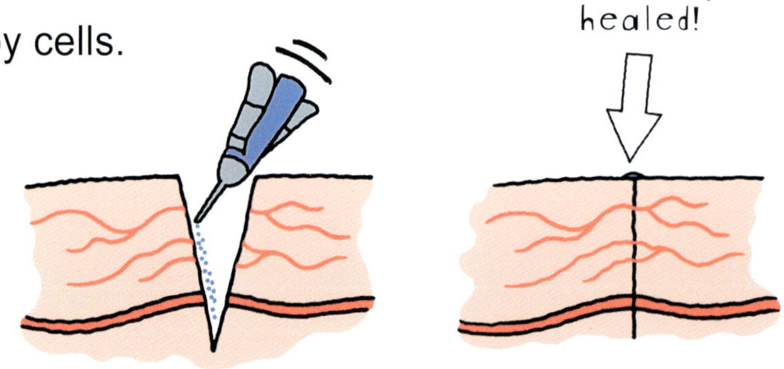

When added up altogether, the silica particles have a very big surface area. This means tiny atomic forces pull them toward the body's cells and toward one another, so the cut closes itself.

Nano masks

Some face masks contain nanofiber filters to trap the tiniest germs.

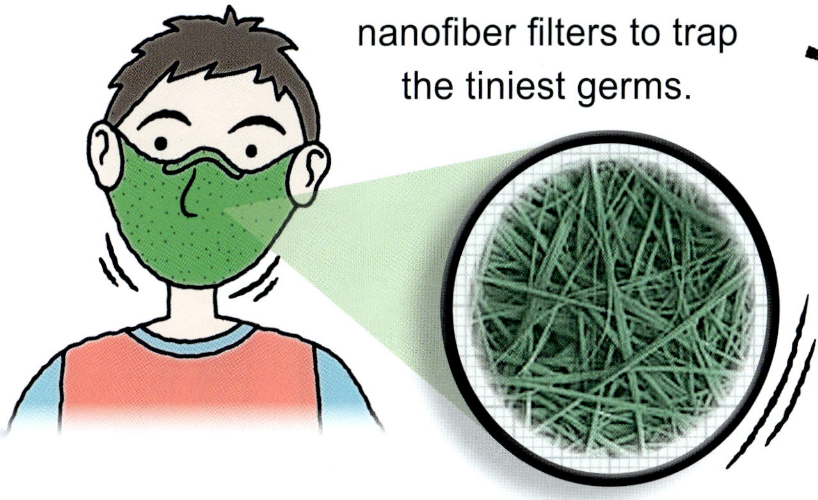

Nano fillings

There are even nanotechnology fillings for teeth. They contain nanoparticles that kill bacteria and rebuild tooth enamel.

Straight to the target!

Using nanotechnology, doctors can target medicines at only the germs or cells they need to reach. They attach a nanoparticle to an antibody – a molecule that sticks to a particular type of germ or cancer cell – and add a molecule of medicine too.

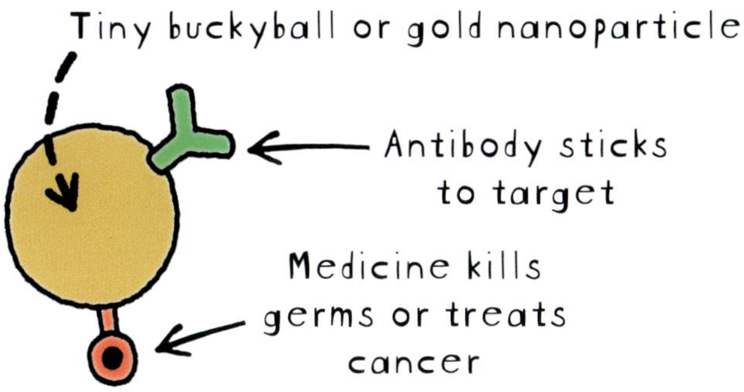

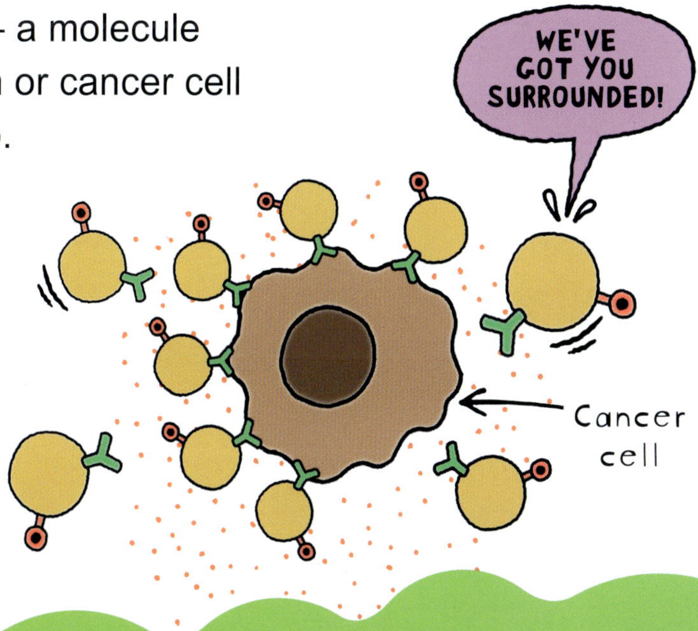

New body parts

Nanomaterials like tough, flexible carbon nanotubes are being used to make extra-strong prosthetic limbs. They can also have graphene skin that can detect touch and graphene solar surfaces that provide an electricity supply.

Nanocomputers

The silicon chips inside today's computers already have nano-sized parts.

Take a typical smartphone, which lots of people have.

Inside is a CPU, or central processing unit – the chip that makes it work.

This chip is less than 0.5 square inch (3.2 sq cm), but contains BILLIONS of tiny transistors!

Each transistor is only about 10 nanometers across.

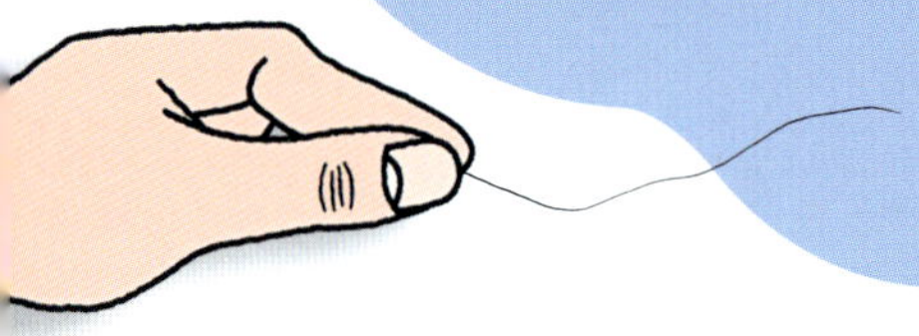

That's so tiny you could fit 8,000 of them into the width of a human hair.

Smaller and smaller?

Chips and transistors have been getting smaller and smaller since they were first invented, over 60 years ago. That's why computers have become smaller and smaller.

But that can't go on forever!

A silicon chip works when electricity flows around it. Electricity flows when tiny electrons jump from one atom to the next.

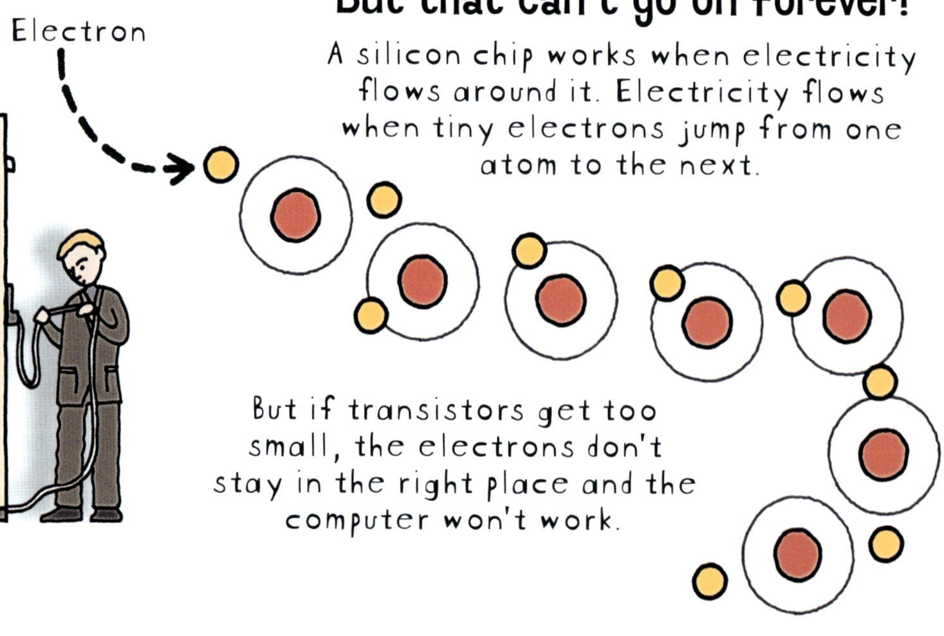

But if transistors get too small, the electrons don't stay in the right place and the computer won't work.

Carbon computing

Instead, scientists are working on making even teenier circuits using carbon nanotubes, which will make computers even smaller and faster.

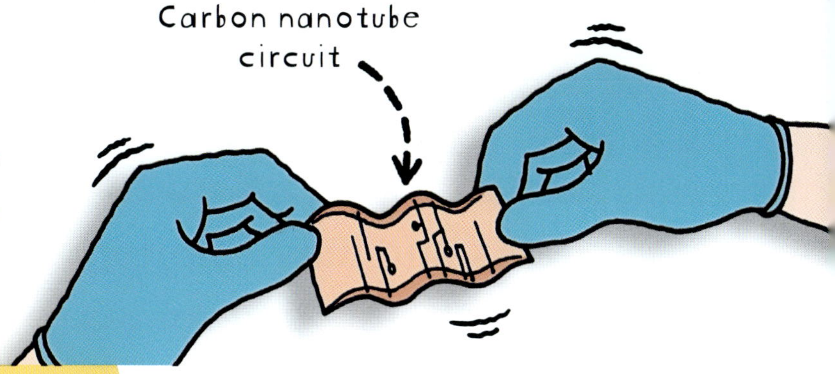

Atomic storage

Computers also have storage chips, where they keep all your files and programs. They're in binary code, made of patterns of 0s and 1s, stored in electronic circuits.

Even though these chips can hold a lot of data, we have **SO MUCH** stuff to store that computers often run out of storage space.

Wearable computers

Carbon nanotube circuits could be used to make super-thin, bendy computers that could be built in to clothes.

Under the microscope

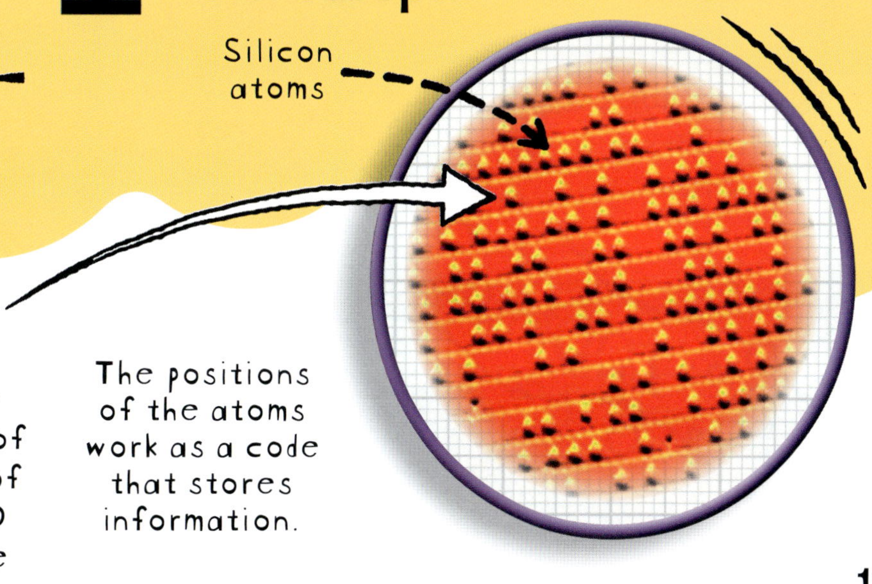

So nanoscientists have come up with a new type of storage, using patterns of atoms. It can store 500 times as much data in the same space.

The positions of the atoms work as a code that stores information.

The nanobots are coming!

Sci-fi books and movies often feature nanobots – tiny robots built from nano-sized parts. They do things like repair damaged cells inside the body or fly around as tiny, invisible spies.

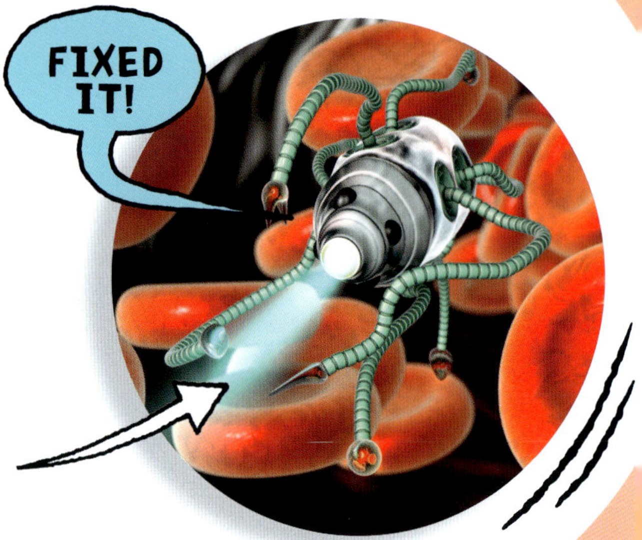

Sci-fi nanobots often look like mini versions of normal robots.

But we're not there yet!

A true robot can move around on its own and be programmed to do a job. That's very hard to do at the nanoscale! Basic nanobots do exist, but they don't look like tiny, shiny metal robots. They're made of molecules and can only do simple jobs.

Here's one that scientists are working on now ...

Nano engine

This tiny engine is made of a silicon dioxide nanotube covered in a chemical that reacts with body chemicals.

In a body liquid such as blood, the chemical reaction makes gas bubbles at one end of the tube. As the bubbles shoot out, they push the nanotube along like a mini rocket.

DNA origami

DNA is a molecule found inside living cells. It contains instructions that make cells work. But DNA can be used in another way. It's long and thin and can be folded into different shapes – a method called "DNA origami."

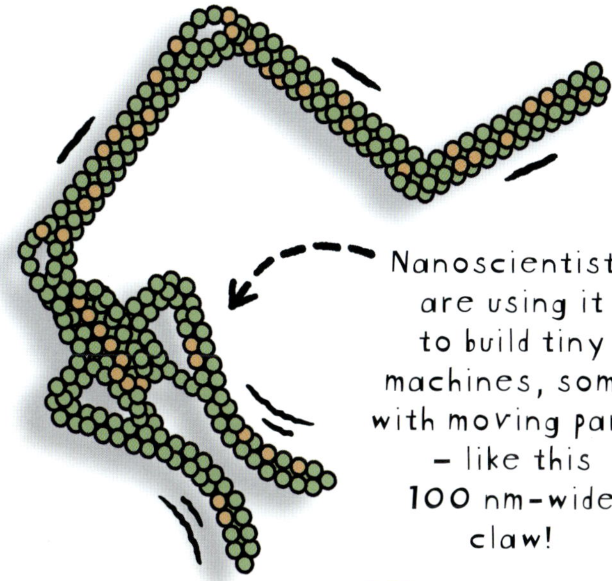

Nanoscientists are using it to build tiny machines, some with moving parts – like this 100 nm-wide claw!

Bot building

Eventually, we could combine robot parts, like the engine and the claw on these pages, to make more advanced nanobots.

Nanobot swarms

Imagine gazillions of nanobots that work together to form different shapes or objects. This idea is called "utility fog."

Scientists have created mini robots that can arrange themselves into different shapes. They're not nano-sized yet but could be in the future.

The bots, called foglets, would link together using tiny arms.

Saving the planet

Our planet faces many environmental problems: pollution, global warming, overpopulation, rising sea levels, and water shortages. Could nanotechnology save the day? Maybe!

Super solar panels

Nanomaterials are helping to make smaller, lighter, and cheaper solar panels to provide clean, green energy from sunlight.

Nanofilters

When cars, factories, and power stations burn fuel, they release harmful soot particles. New nanomaterial filters can catch these particles and stop them from escaping.

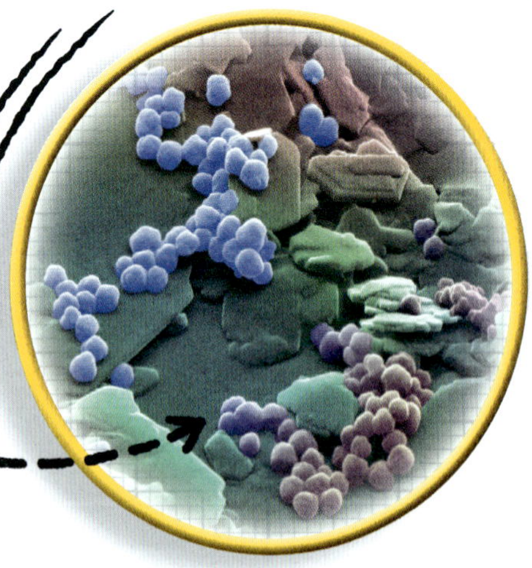

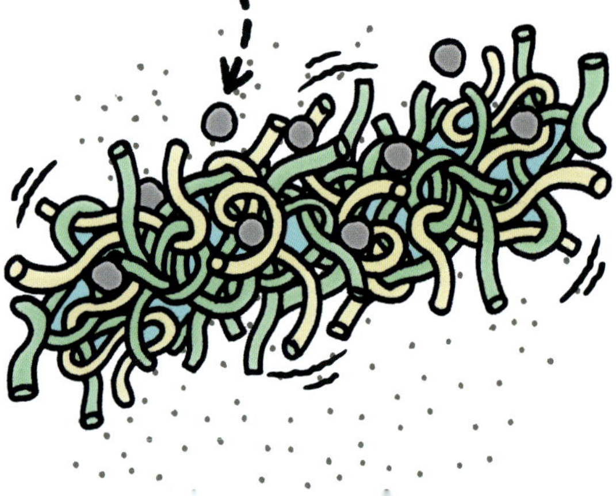

Some can even remove sea salt, to turn seawater into drinking water. This could be very useful if climate change causes water shortages.

Recycle it!

Soot particles from burning fuel contain carbon. And what's carbon good for?

Nanomaterials!

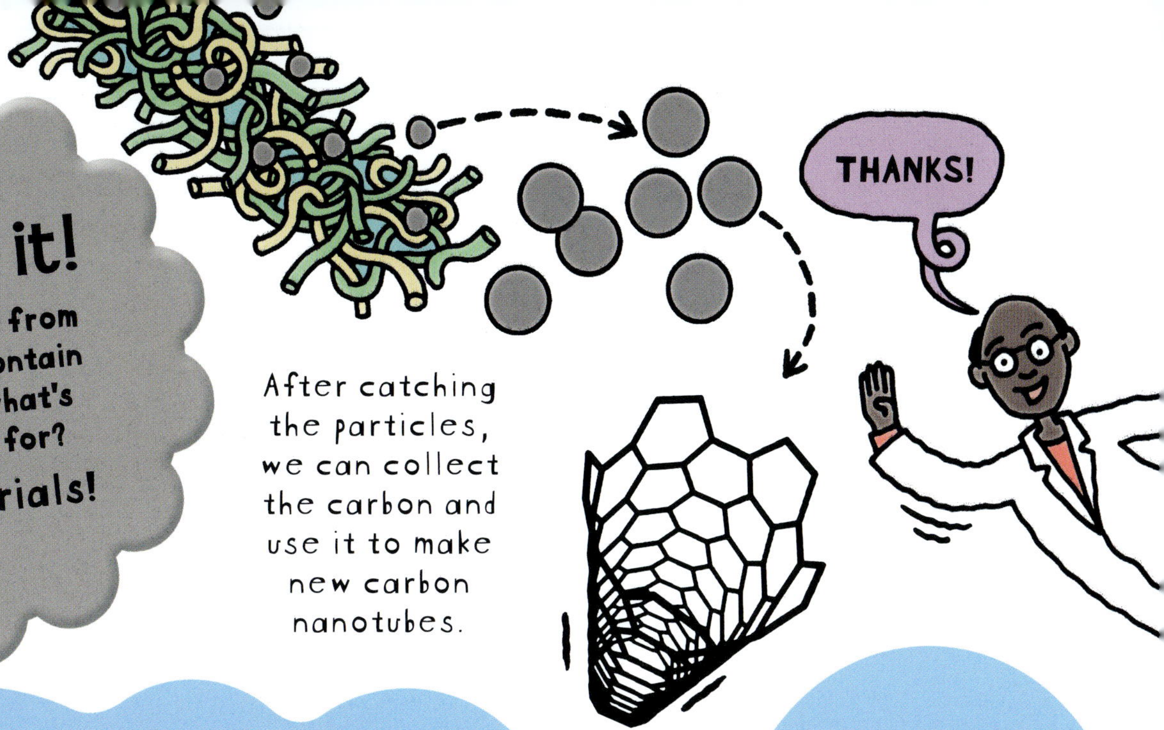

After catching the particles, we can collect the carbon and use it to make new carbon nanotubes.

Global cooling

Burning fuels also releases carbon dioxide gas. It traps heat in the atmosphere, causing global warming. Could we use nanotechnology to take carbon dioxide out of the air?

Trees and plants do this naturally. They take in carbon dioxide and water and use energy from sunlight to turn them into food. We are planting more trees but they take years to grow.

So nanoscientists have designed a genius artificial leaf to help out.

What could possibly go wrong?

Nanotechnology could do all kinds of amazing and useful things ...

but is it safe?

Breathing them in

Breathing in tiny particles can harm your lungs – especially long, thin fibers. For example, asbestos is made of tiny fibers and can cause deadly lung diseases. Some nanomaterials, like nanotubes, are a similar shape.

Under the microscope

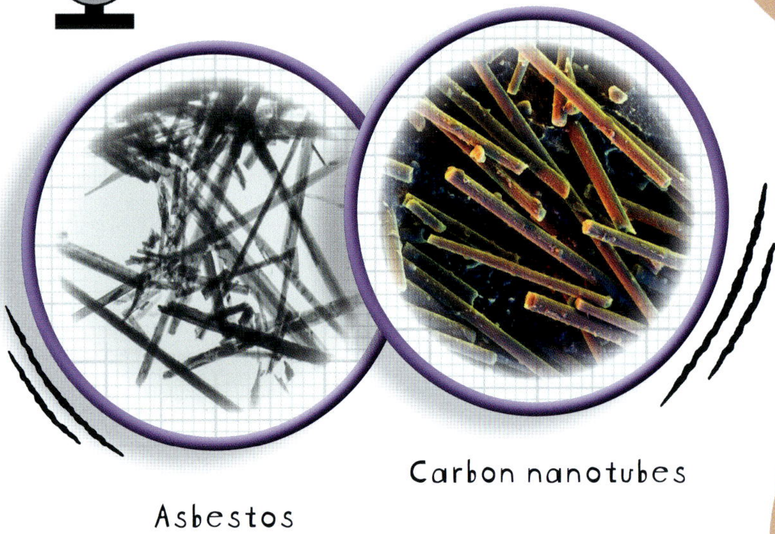

Asbestos

Carbon nanotubes

Some scientists think carbon nanotubes could damage our lungs – but no one's sure yet! We have to keep doing safety tests and checks to find out.

Nano pollution

Tiny particles of plastic and soot cause harmful pollution. In fact, nanotechnology is being used to clean them up (see page 14). But nanoparticles themselves could also be a problem for the environment.

Take silver nanoparticles, used in socks and bandages to kill harmful bacteria, for example ...

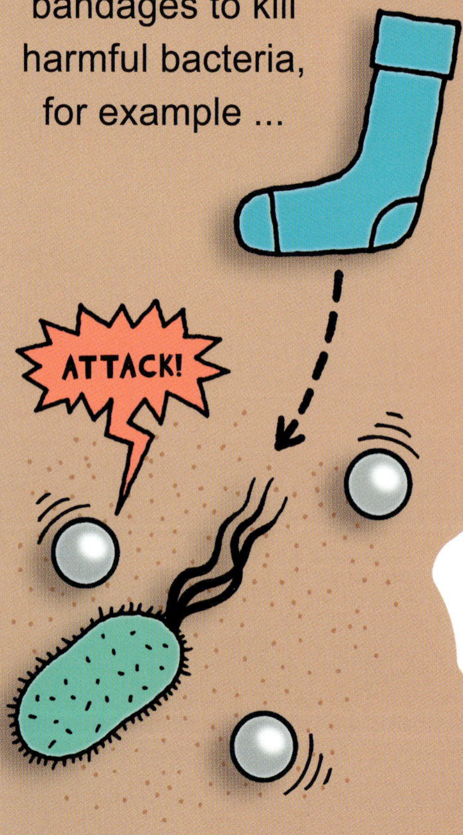

If they escape into the environment, the silver particles can end up killing other bacteria, too, including healthy bacteria in the soil, for example.

Because of this, we might have to stop using nanosilver or find a way to make it safer.

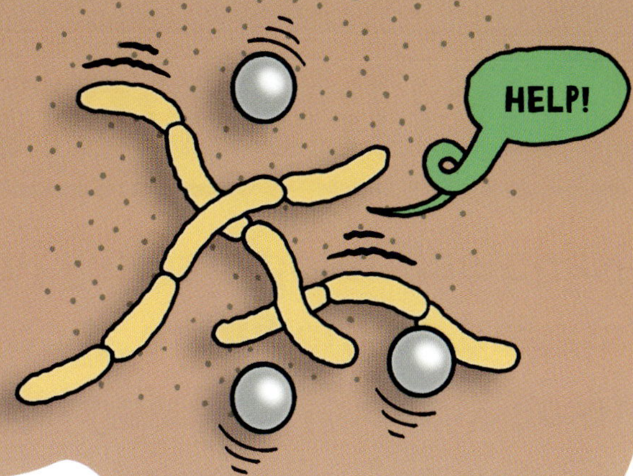

Safety in the lab

Working in a nanotechnology lab could be dangerous. You could breathe in or swallow harmful nanoparticles.

So, nanotechnologists sometimes wear protective gear, like this.

Nano explosions

Some tiny particles, including flour and coal dust, can form a cloud in the air that explodes easily. Nanoparticles can do this too. So, it's important to control lab experiments carefully to stop nanodust from escaping.

Grey goo nightmare

An even worse fear is that one day, nanobots could copy themselves, using the materials around them to make more and more and **MORE** nanobots. They could turn the whole world into a pile of nanobots, known as **GREY GOO**.

But DON'T PANIC!

Luckily, scientists think this isn't really possible. Phew!

Future nanotech

Nanotechnology is only just getting started. In the future, it could lead to all kinds of amazing inventions we can only dream of today …

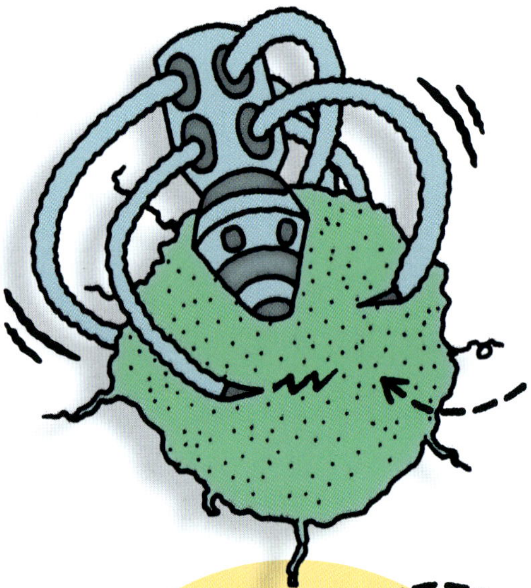

Permanent medical nanobots that live inside you, cleaning up any pollution you've breathed in and zapping germs and diseases as soon as they appear.

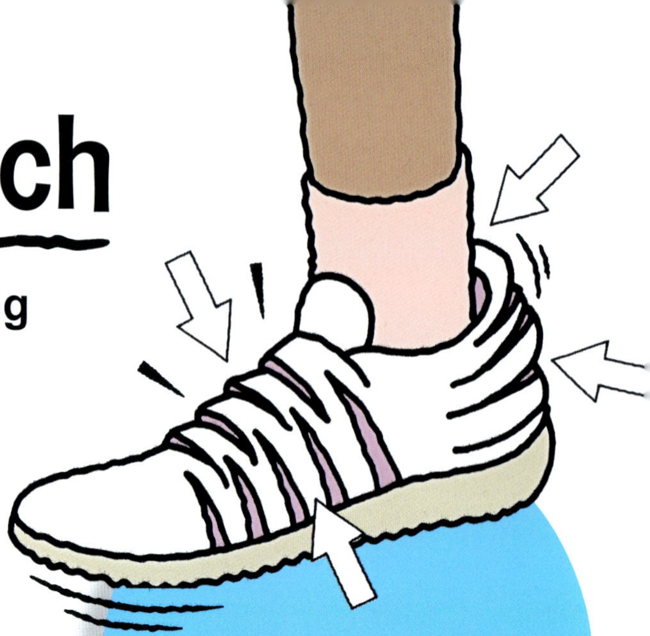

Shoes that adjust their size and shape to fit you perfectly.

Self-cleaning clothes, toys, plates and cups, bikes, floors – everything!

Utility fog exoskeletons that can fly or give you extra strength or abilities.

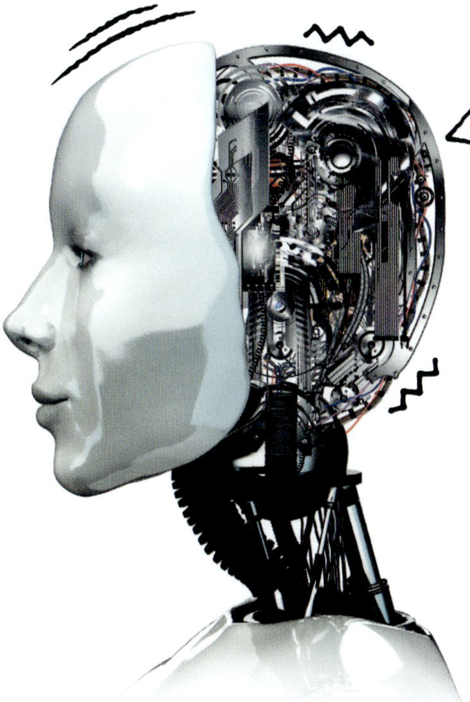

Nanowire computer circuits that work in 3D – like our own brains – growing, changing, and learning as they process new information.

Maybe a future robot could have a nanotech brain ... but would we really want it to?!

Pet food additives that turn pet poop into harmless, safe chemicals.

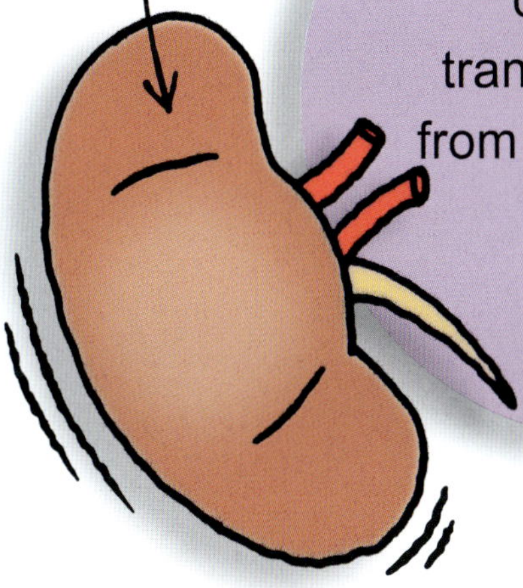

Replacement organs for transplants, built from scratch, atom by atom.

Or even a space elevator linking Earth to a space station, built using super-strong, light graphene.

What else?

You can probably think of loads more ideas too. In fact, if you like nanotechnology, you could consider doing it as a job and put your ideas into practice.

How tiny?

Things that measure on the nanoscale are incredibly tiny – so small, it's hard to imagine them. On this page, you can see the sizes of some of the things in this book, compared to one another.

Micro measures

For measuring normal everyday things, we use centimeters, inches, meters, or feet.

For tiny things like cells, scientists use a smaller measurement – the micron or micrometer.

It's 1 thousandth of a millimeter. The micron symbol is:

µm

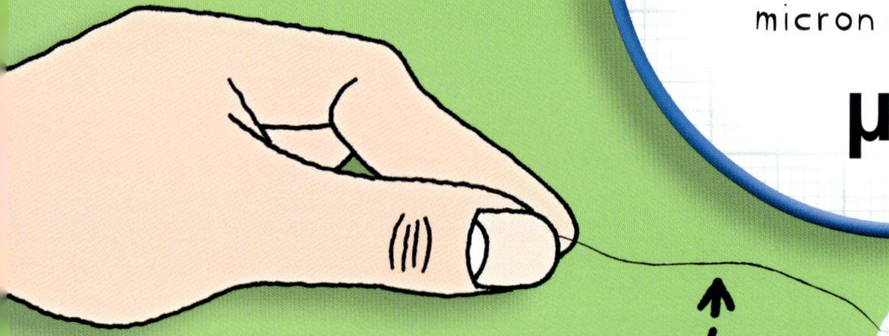

A human hair, for example, is around 80 µm thick.

And at the nanoscale, they use the even teenier nanometer, which is 1 thousandth of a micron, or 1 millionth of a millimeter.

The nanometer symbol is:

nm

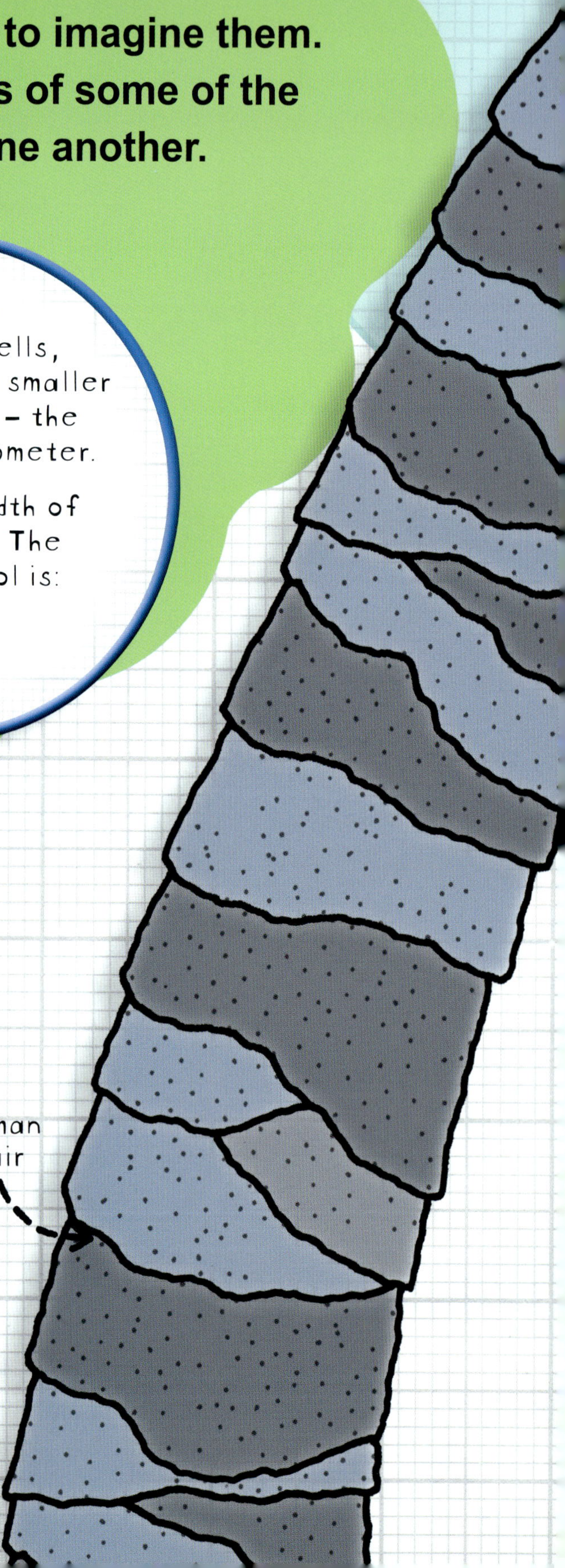

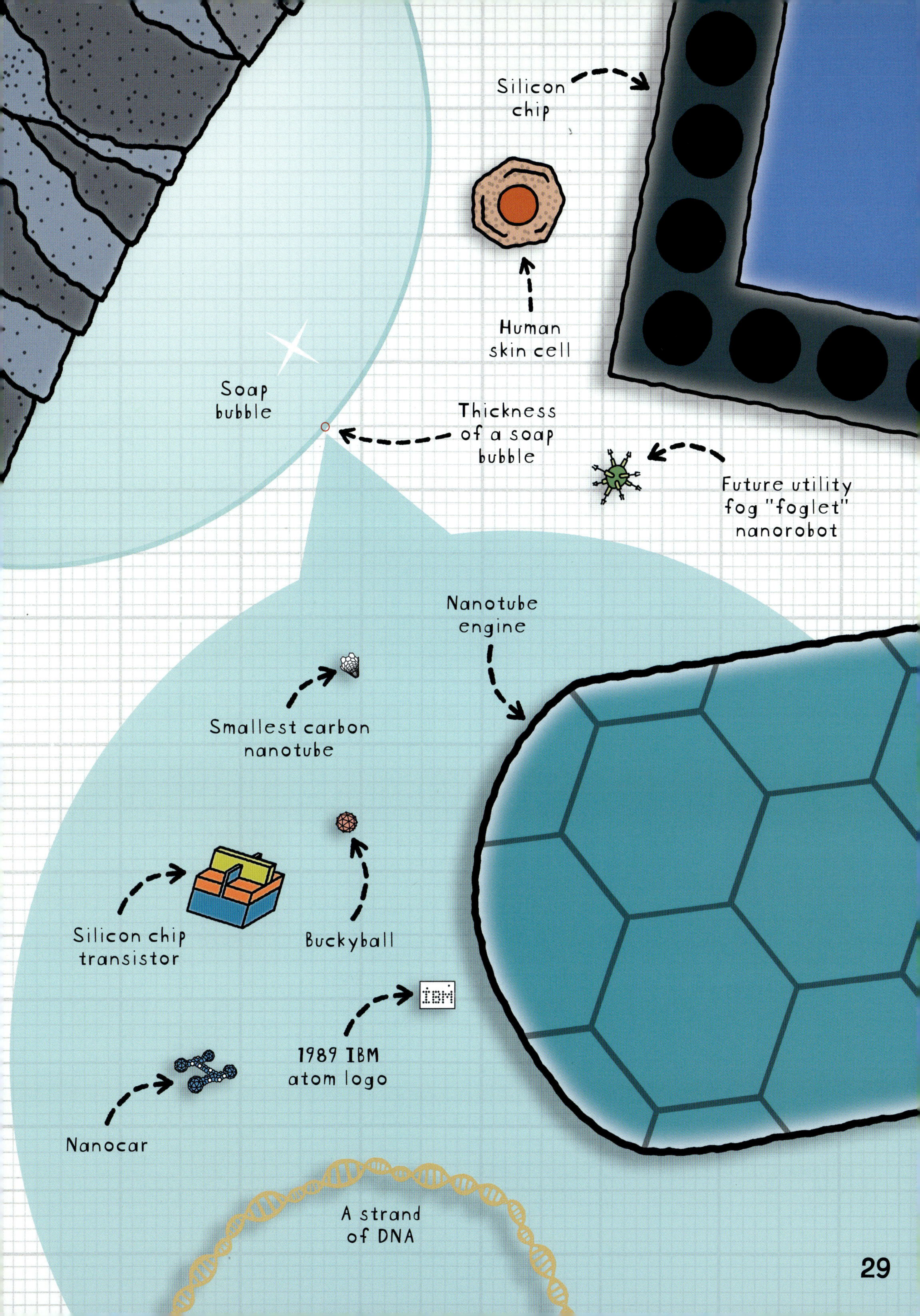
Silicon chip
Human skin cell
Soap bubble
Thickness of a soap bubble
Future utility fog "foglet" nanorobot
Nanotube engine
Smallest carbon nanotube
Silicon chip transistor
Buckyball
IBM
1989 IBM atom logo
Nanocar
A strand of DNA

Glossary

atoms The tiny units that all matter is made up of.

buckyball A ball-shaped nanoparticle made from carbon atoms.

carbon A common element found in living things and often used to make nanomaterials.

carbon dioxide A gas found in the air that plants take in during photosynthesis.

cells The tiny building blocks that make up living things.

DNA (Short for deoxyribonucleic acid) A string-shaped chemical found inside cells.

electronic circuit A circuit that uses the flow of electricity to do calculations or store information.

electrons Tiny particles that zoom around on the outer edge of atoms.

elements Pure materials made of only one type of atom.

foglets A name for the individual nanobots that could make up utility fog in the future.

global warming An increase in Earth's average temperature caused by human activities.

graphene A type of nanofilm, or very thin film, made from carbon atoms.

graphite A mineral made from carbon and used to make pencils.

grey goo A name for an out-of-control mass of countless nanobots.

laser A device that uses atoms to make a narrow beam of light of a single color.

materials Different types of matter, or stuff.

micrometer Another name for a micron.

micron A tiny unit of measurement, 1/1000th of a millimeter long.

mineral A pure, natural, non-living, solid substance.

molecules Units of matter made from atoms joined together.

nanobot A nanoscale robot.

nanocar A nanoscale working model car.

nanoclay A clay-like material containing nanoparticles.

nanofilms Flat layers of material with a thickness on the nanoscale.

nanofilter A filter for removing impurities, made using nanomaterials.

nanomaterials Materials that are on the nanoscale in one or more dimensions, or materials that have nanoscale features.

nanomedicine Medical treatments that use nanotechnology.

nanometer A tiny unit of measurement, one-millionth of a millimeter long.

nanoparticles Tiny speck-like nanomaterials.

nanopillars Nanoscale spikes or sticking-out parts on a surface.

nanorobot Another word for a nanobot.

nanoscale Between 1 and 100 nanometers in size.

nanotechnologist A scientist or engineer working in nanotechnology.

nanotubes Tiny string or tube-shaped nanomaterials.

nanowires Another name for nanotubes.

organ A body part that does a special job, such as the stomach, liver, heart, or kidneys.

organelles Small parts inside a cell that act like miniature body organs to do different jobs.

oxygen A gas found in the air on Earth that humans and other animals need to breathe to stay alive.

particle A tiny part.

prosthetic limb An artificial replacement arm or leg.

scanning tunneling microscope (STM) A microscope that uses a fine tip to sense or move atoms.

silicon A common element often used in nanotechnology.

silicon chip A tiny electronic circuit printed on to a small piece of silicon.

solar panel A panel of material that turns energy from sunlight into a flow of electricity.

transistor A part in an electronic circuit that controls or changes the flow of information.

utility fog A proposed future material made up of millions of nanorobots, or "foglets," that could assemble themselves into different shapes and objects.

vacuum tube A part that works like a transistor, used in early computers.

wind turbine A device that uses the movement of wind to turn large blades and then converts the turning movement into a flow of electricity.

Further information

Websites

www.nanowerk.com/n_neatstuff.php

Activities, pictures, games, and facts from the Nanowerk nanotechnology hub.

www.nanooze.org

Nanooze, a site with science and nanotech news and activities for kids.

www.mrsec.psu.edu/content/nano-activities-kids

Fun nano-activities from Penn State University's Center for Nanoscale Science.

www.youtube.com/watch?v=oSCX78-8-qO&t=12s

"A Boy and His Atom," an animation made with atoms from IBM.

home.cern/resources/video/physics/voyage-world-atoms

Amazing video zooming in to look at the nanoscale and atoms, from CERN atomic lab.

Books

Nano: The Spectacular Science of the Very (Very) Small

By Dr. Jess Wade and Melissa Castrillón (Walker Books, 2021)

Microcosmos: Discovering the World Through Microscopic Images

By Brandon Broll (Firefly Books, 2010)

Discover Nanotechnology

By Lisa J. Amstutz (Lerner Publishing Group, 2017)

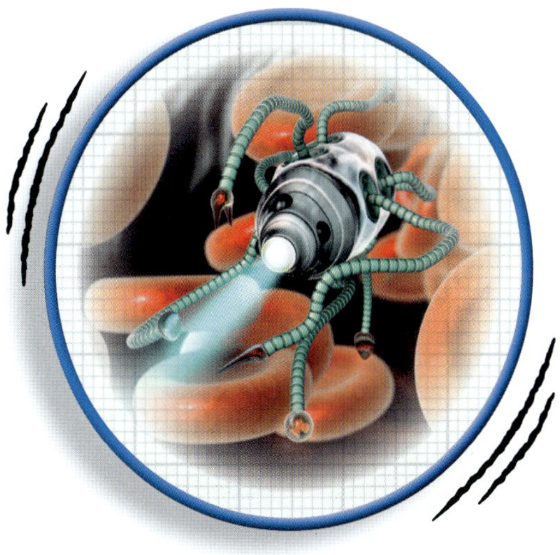

Every effort has been made by the Publishers to ensure that the websites in this book are suitable for children, that they are of the highest educational value, and that they contain no inappropriate or offensive material. However, because of the nature of the Internet, it is impossible to guarantee that the contents of these sites will not be altered. We strongly advise that Internet access is supervised by a responsible adult.

Index